EARTH'S FIERY FURY

EARTH'S FIERY FURY

SANDRA DOWNS

TWENTY-FIRST CENTURY BOOKS
BROOKFIELD, CONNECTICUT

To Mom and Dad, for their love and support

Library of Congress Cataloging-in-Publication Data
Downs, Sandra.
Earth's fiery fury / Sandra Downs.
p. cm. — (Exploring planet earth)
Includes bibliographical references and index.
Summary: Explains such dynamic forces of nature as volcanoes, fumaroles,
hot springs, and geysers.
ISBN 0-7613-1413-X (lib. bdg.)
1. Volcanoes—Juvenile literature. 2. Geothermal resources—Juvenile literature.
[1. Volcanoes. 2. Geothermal resources.] I. Title.
QE521.3.D68 2000 551.21—dc21 00-024956

Published by Twenty-First Century Books
A Division of The Millbrook Press, Inc.
2 Old New Milford Road
Brookfield, Connecticut 06804
www.millbrookpress.com

Copyright © 2000 by Sandra Downs
Printed in the United States of America
All rights reserved
5 4 3 2 1

Cover photograph courtesy of Liaison Agency (© Kevin West)
Photographs courtesy of J. Warren, 1990: p. 9; Liaison Agency: pp. 12 (© Marc Deville), 17
(© Adventurier/Loviny), 20 (© Richard Elkins), 48 (© Bill Cardoni), 51 (left: © Gisli Hrafnsson), 51 (right);
Bruce Coleman, Inc.: pp. 13 (© N. O. Tomalin), 26 (© Arthur M. Greene), 33 (© Kenneth Fink); Photo
Researchers, Inc./Science Source: pp. 14 (© Stephen and Donna O'Meara), 27 (© Dr. Ken MacDonald), 37
(© Stephen and Donna O'Meara), 44 (G. R. Roberts Photo Library), 55 (© Bernhard Edmaier/SPL); Woodfin
Camp & Associates: pp. 16 (© Gary Braasch), 18 (© Gary Braasch); National Geophysical Data Center: pp.
19 (R. I. Meyers), 32 (H. Schmincke); Photo Researchers, Inc./National Audubon Society Collection: pp. 25
(© William W. Bacon III), 38 (left: © Linda Bartlett, right: © Francois Gohier), 40 (© Brenda Tharp);
U. S. Geological Survey: pp. 28 (J. D. Griggs/HVO 75cp), 29 (J. W. Vallance/MSH-7-22-80 Erupt. 58ct), 30
(M. T. Mangan), 39 (T. J. Takahashi/HVO 104cp); National Park Service: p. 31 (Cecil W. Stoughton), 52
(W. S. Keller); NGS Image Collection: pp. 42 (© Norbert Rosing), 47 (© Raymond Gehman); Alexander
Turnbull Library, National Library of New Zealand, Te Puna Mātauranga o Aotearoa: p. 45

CONTENTS

EARTH'S FIERY FURY

Broken into huge pieces like a jigsaw puzzle, the earth's surface is constantly in motion. Known as tectonic plates, these pieces float on top of a vast reservoir of molten material deep inside the earth. These tectonic plates carry along big chunks of the earth's crust—often including entire oceans and continents.

Slowly floating on top of a vast zone of soft, semiliquid rock, the tectonic plates slip and crunch into each other. In the deepest depths of the Pacific Ocean, the edges of several plates slip under or over each other in an area called the sub-duction zone. Here, chunks of the earth's crust melt into magma—liquid rock—as one tectonic plate dives under another.

The ash from the 1989 eruption of Mount Redoubt, Alaska, nearly caused KLM flight 867 to crash on its way to Anchorage.

On the other side of the earth, tectonic plates pull apart from each other along the mid-Atlantic ridge. As the seafloor spreads, magma bubbles through the gap and hardens in the cold water, widening the Atlantic Ocean's floor by 1 inch (2.5 centimeters) or more each year.

Along the edges of these plates, and in certain hot spots around the planet, superheated magma shoots upward. Forcing its way through weak rock, it melts and churns until it finds a vent where it can spurt out on the surface. When magma reaches the earth's surface—pouring out of the ground or bursting forth in a violent eruption—we call the spot a volcano.

Volcanic activity creates new land. Volcanoes spit out lava from their vents, and rain down ash and rocks on the surrounding countryside. Some volcanic formations, like fumaroles, hot springs, and geysers, seem almost alive. They sputter puffs of steam, gurgle with superheated water, and belch smelly clouds of sulfur dioxide.

These dynamic forces of nature remind us that our earth is constantly in a state of change. Magma seethes and bubbles to create new land, to form new rocks, and to burst forth in tremendous displays of the earth's fiery fury.

1

VULCAN'S FURNACE

In A.D. 79, the Roman naturalist and historian Pliny the Younger watched from the city of Misenum as a disaster unfolded. His written record gives us the earliest glimpse into the fury of a volcanic eruption.

> The black cloud seemed to descend and enshroud
> the whole ocean . . . the ashes began to fall . . .
> darkness overspread us. Not the darkness of a
> cloudy night, or when there is no moon, but that of
> a chamber, which is closed shut.

Three days and nights fire drizzled down from the blackened peak. Colorful vapors lit the sky with unusual colors: blood red, emerald green, sickly yellow. Explosions sent clouds of gas and ash high into the atmosphere, dropping a rain of hot boulders as large as houses. The ground shook with terrible earthquakes. The sea drew back from the shore, then hurled itself in a giant wave toward the mountain. Some people ran from the mountain in terror. Others hid in their cellars. On the third day, the mountain erupted. A mass of hot gases and ash rolled over the cities, followed by a flood of steaming mud.

Restoration work on one of the bodies at Pompeii

In the nearby cities of Pompeii and Herculaneum, people tried to flee. Some escaped. But the mud and the ash buried most of them, to be forever frozen in stone.

PLAYING WITH FIRE

More than a million people now live within the shadow of Mount Vesuvius in Italy. Its eruption in A.D. 79 engulfed the cities of Pompeii and Herculaneum in moments. In 1631, a wall of lava poured down the mountain, burying as many as 18,000 people. In 1707, the skies in Naples, 200 miles (322 kilometers) away, turned black as midnight from a rain of ash. Since Pliny the Younger described its wrath, Vesuvius has erupted at least fifty times. Volcanologists—geologists who specialize in volcanoes—keep careful watch over the constant rumblings of this dangerous volcano. They wait for a sign, any sign, to give them the confidence to order an evacuation, and to avoid panicking people with a false alarm. With a million lives at stake, Vesuvius is a disaster waiting to happen—again.

Italy has a long history of living with volcanoes. Stromboli, in the Lipari Islands, is nicknamed the Lighthouse of the Mediterranean. It's been erupting continuously for more than 2,000 years. Every twenty minutes or so, it throws glowing ashes into the sky. Mount Etna, on the eastern coast of Sicily, erupted regularly during the Middle Ages. It still pours massive lava flows into the cities at its base. And the smoldering isle of Vulcano, off the northern coast of Sicily, was thought to be the home of Vulcan,

KICK 'EM, JENNY!

Since 1939, it's been taunting sailors with boiling seas and belching smoke. It throws rocks up out of an otherwise calm sea. Kick 'Em Jenny, a seamount just off the coast of Grenada, is closer to the ocean's surface than any other seamount in the world. Someday soon, it will break through the waves and become the newest island in the Caribbean.

All of the world's island arcs are volcanic and were once seamounts, such as Japan, the Lesser Antilles (Caribbean), the Mariana Islands (South Pacific), the Aleutian Islands (Alaska), and the Hawaiian Islands.

The island of Surtsey, off southern Iceland, rose from the ocean in 1963 and was made into a nature preserve in 1965.

the Roman god of fire. According to Roman mythology, Vulcan served as blacksmith to the gods, forging tools and weapons in the reddish glow of a forge. His workshop belched smoke and sulfur fumes—and his name gives us the word "volcano."

Mythology and ancient religions use the volcano as a symbol of sacred, mysterious power. The Greeks believed that Typhon, a fear-

Mount Bromo in the Tengger Mountains, East Java, Indonesia

some hundred-headed monster, caused the rumblings inside Mount Etna. In Mexico, the Aztecs worshiped volcanoes, leaving sacrifices to appease the volcano gods. Living under the flickering slopes of Mauna Loa, the Hawaiians invoked Madam Pele, a vengeful goddess. And in Japan, people revere Fujiyama—the sacred, never-dying mountain—because of its symmetrical shape.

But why do people choose to live near such dangerous mountains? Volcanic slopes attract settlers because volcanoes create the most fertile soil on earth. Magma contains all the crucial chemicals necessary for plant growth. Ash generated by a volcanic eruption, made up of tiny bits of volcanic glass, breaks down into soil within months. Loaded with phosphorous, potassium, calcium, magnesium, and sulfur, this soil provides plants with all the nutrients they need. Lush crops grow on the slopes of Mount Vesuvius, feeding millions of people. There are vineyards, orchards, and thousands of vegetable gardens. It's the best farmland in Italy.

In Java, home of many explosively erupting volcanoes, farmers treasure the fertile soil. Thanks to the rich soil and the wet, steamy climate, they can grow as many as three crops of rice every year. On the Caribbean islands, flat stretches of volcanic soil hold productive sugarcane fields. In Hawaii, pineapples and sugarcane grow in soils created by volcanic ash. Around the world, more than five hundred million people live on land once covered with fiery lava, or near a dormant volcano. But since most volcanoes erupt intermittently—and not very frequently, compared to our life spans—many people don't even consider living near a volcano a danger. The benefit of living on volcanic soil outweighs the risk.

BUILDING NEW LANDSCAPES

Some mountain ranges owe their birth to volcanic action. Uplifting along the edge of a tectonic plate, the Rocky Mountains and the Andes contain sharp-topped extinct volcanoes, quiet dormant volcanoes, and peaks that still smolder with the potential of eruption. The Cascade Range, extending from California to Washington, has at least fourteen snow-capped peaks that could suddenly erupt, as Mount St. Helens did in 1980.

Volcanoes come in many shapes and sizes. Helgafell, in Iceland, is only 725 feet (221 meters) tall. Mount Kilamanjaro in Africa, a snow-capped dormant volcano, is 19,340 feet (5,895 meters) tall. Cotopaxi, in Ecuador, is an active volcano almost 20,000 feet (6,096 meters) tall. And the world's tallest mountain isn't Mount Everest—it's Mauna Loa! This active Hawaiian volcano rises more than 30,000 feet (9,144 meters) from the deep seafloor of the Pacific Ocean, with only 13,680 feet (4,170 meters) of the volcano sticking out above sea level.

The depths of the world's oceans hide most of our planet's volcanoes—nearly 20,000 of them, called seamounts. They form along fissures in the seafloor near the edges of tectonic plates and

The Cascade Range has many volcanoes that might erupt at any moment.

over hot spots where plumes of magma rise like fountains from exceptionally hot regions in the earth's mantle. Silent and unseen in their submarine world, seamounts constantly build upward from the ocean floor. Because of the depth of the ocean, many seamounts rival the height of volcanoes on the earth's surface. Eventually, they pop through the surface of the ocean, and we stop calling them seamounts. They become islands.

Few people see a seamount turn into an island. But in 1957, off the Azores, islands in the eastern Atlantic Ocean, a ship's captain watched as the sea boiled and turned red.

According to depth charts, he thought he moored his ship in 300 feet (91 meters) of water. So he moved the ship and set anchor again. The crew continued to watch as steam and lava bubbled out of the sea. Less than a day later, a tiny island emerged.

Today, geologists use seismographs to pinpoint undersea eruptions. In 1996, tremors led scientists to re-investigate Loihi, a volcano rising 9,000 feet (2,743 meters) from the ocean floor 21 miles (34 kilometers) off the coast of Hawaii. Using sonar, they discovered that Loihi, with its cone still 3,000 feet (914 meters) beneath the waves, had blown its top. As it continues to grow, Loihi will become the next island (and the seventh volcano) in the Hawaiian islands—in about fifty thousand years or so.

The biggest eruption in recorded history was at Mount Tambora, Indonesia, in 1815. Its "big bang" was heard 970 miles (1,561 kilometers) away! The explosion threw a 19.2-cubic-mile (80-cubic-kilometer) cloud of dust into the atmosphere. Gases mixed with water vapor caused sulfuric acid to fall from the skies. Ten thousand people died instantly. During the following year, more than eighty thousand people died as a result of famine brought on by cold weather created by the dust cloud.

The "loudest noise ever heard" happened in 1883 when Mount Krakatau, an island in the Sunda Straits of Indonesia, blew its top. People heard the explosion in Alice Springs, Australia, 2,000 miles (3,219 kilometers) away and on the Isle of Rodriquez in the Indian Ocean, more than 3,000 miles (4,827 kilometers) away. More than 4.3 cubic miles (18 cubic kilometers) of ash rose into the atmosphere from the eruption. The force of the explosion created a tsunami 100 feet (30.5 meters) high, drowning 36,000 people on the adjoining Indonesian islands of Java and Sumatra.

In 1991, one of the largest volcanic eruptions of the twentieth century occurred when Mount Pinatubo, in the Philippines, blew its top. The eruptive cloud rose 19 miles (30 kilometers) into the sky, and contained 1.2 cubic miles (5 cubic kilometers) of ash and 22

Mudflows from Mount Pinatubo's eruption buried entire villages.

megatons (20 metric megatons) of sulfur dioxide. The volcano threw so many particles into the atmosphere that the average air temperature dropped 2°F (-16°C).

Nearly 600,000 years ago, a tremendous eruption blew apart the bedrock of the Yellowstone Valley. This explosion, at least ten times as strong as the one at Mount Tambora, threw a thick blanket of volcanic dust over western North America. What remains is a crater 45 miles (28 kilometers) long, 30 miles (48 kilometers) wide. The crater's more than 200 hot springs and geysers are fed by water that is heated by pools of 427°F (800°C) magma, 3 miles (5 kilometers) below the earth's surface.

TYPES OF VOLCANOES

Some volcanoes, like Mauna Loa and Stromboli, erupt constantly. Others awaken from long periods of slumber with a huge, unexpected blast. And still others have never erupted—but they might. So how do we know if a volcano is active, dormant, or extinct?

The U.S. Geological Survey (USGS) defines an active volcano as one that has had an eruption in the past 2,000 years—that is, within the scope of recorded human history. But since written accounts vary from several hundred years in the Pacific Northwest to thousands of years in Europe and Asia, this isn't a perfect definition. Dormant volcanoes show some signs of volcanic activity, such as a buildup of gases in the soil or the venting of steam through fumaroles, but they aren't known to ever have erupted before. And extinct volcanoes, in the Auvergne region of France, show geologic signs of having erupted at least once, but they are never expected to erupt again.

The basalt cliffs of Horse Thief Butte, along the Columbia River Gorge in Washington

Based on their style of eruption, which is driven by the nature of the magma pouring out of the vents, volcanoes fit into several categories.

Shield volcanoes like Mauna Loa, in Hawaii, erupt like a pot boiling over. Basaltic lava steadily flows out of the volcano's many vents. As the fiery rivers of lava cool, they build up huge mounds of hardened lava. The largest mountains on earth are extinct shield volcanoes.

Fissure volcanoes (also called Icelandic volcanoes) are a specialized type of shield volcano. Runny lava pours out from fissures in the ground. These volcanoes can be miles long, spreading lava again and again in wide sheets across flat plains. Geologists theorize that the 100,000-square-mile (59,000-square-kilometer) Columbia River plateau—a sheet of basalt covering much of Oregon and Washington—formed in such a manner, as did many other spots on earth referred to as "flood basalts."

When **cinder cone volcanoes** erupt, they throw clots or jets of thick and sticky basaltic lava into the air by explosions of gas within the magma pipe. The lava cools, falling as cinders, and builds

In California, on March 22, 1915, Mount Lassen erupted. A series of eruptions from 1914 to 1915 caused mudflows and lahars that swept 31 miles (50 kilometers) down the valleys of Hat and Lost Creeks.

a steep cone-shaped hill around the main vent. These volcanoes grow rapidly and often grow in clusters, often with a lava flow erupting from their base as well. Cinder cones like Paricutin, in Mexico, are the most common kinds of volcanoes.

Composite volcanoes have two different types of eruptions. Thick, pasty lava oozes out of the crater, forming lava flows. Explosive eruptions add layers of ash and rock on top of the lava flows, and the cycle repeats itself, building the volcano like a layer cake. Many of the world's snow-capped peaks, including Mount Ranier, in Washington, and Mount Fuji, in Japan, are dormant or extinct composite volcanoes.

Dome volcanoes form as lava rises from the vent like toothpaste squished out of a tube, then hardens in place. Lassen Peak,

Mount Lassen, in northern California, is the focus of Lassen Volcanic National Park.

in California, is a lava dome—one of the largest in the world. If gases trapped behind the dome build up to an explosive peak, they can blow a hole through the dome in a massive eruption.

VOLCANIC ERUPTIONS

The nature of magma helps us define types of volcanic eruptions. Magma can be very thick and gooey or very runny—and everything in between. Gases inside the magma affect how violent the eruption may be.

Hawaiian eruptions occur when shield or fissure volcanoes bubble over, pouring out rivers of fluid hot lava. When the eruptions start, gassy jets spurt lava into the air, creating fountains of "fire." Kilauea and Mauna Loa have these types of eruptions.

Strombolian eruptions are named after Stromboli, in Italy. Puffy white vapor clouds of steam and hot gases rise from the cone. The thick, viscous magma is filled with gas bubbles. Bursting bub-

VOLCANOLOGY

The first descriptions of volcanoes came from the early Greeks. Aristotle defined a volcano as "wind striking fire from seams of sulfur and coal." After visiting the volcanoes of Rome, the historian Strabo called them "open orifices whereby fire, ignited matter, and water escape." Pliny the Elder, historian and observer of the A.D. 79 eruption of Mount Vesuvius, gave extremely detailed descriptions of the eruption.

Over the ages, geologists and other scientists attempted to understand the origins of rocks by identifying how they related to the rocks found around volcanoes. Other people, among them Benjamin Franklin, noted how the weather seemed to be affected by volcanic eruptions. But it wasn't until 1902 that the serious study of volcanoes began. After Mount Pelée erupted, erasing the city of St. Pierre, Martinique, geologist Alfred Lacroix spent the next year learning everything he could about the volcano. His detailed report explaining the dynamic forces interacting to form an eruption became the foundation of the new science of volcanology.

Volcanologists study the effects of ancient eruptions by analyzing the geology around a volcano. Different types of eruptions leave behind different types of rock. Volcanologists also continuously monitor the changes in some dormant and active volcanoes. Well before a dormant volcano springs to life, it "breathes" gases into the ground. Carbon dioxide and sulfur dioxide seep into the air. Volcanologists use special instruments to measure these gases. And as the magma builds up in chambers below the volcano, pressure can cause tremors and earthquakes. Volcanologists use seismographs to measure the intensity of tremors, and tiltmeters and geodimeters to measure the subtle swelling of a volcano as it "breathes," or expands.

As volcanologists continue to learn more about volcanoes, they've become more skilled at forecasting eruptions. But monitoring volcanoes is expensive— and dangerous. Many volcanologists have died studying volcanoes. And sometimes the volcano fools the volcanologists. Magma rises up the pipe more quickly than expected, or solidifies in place, throwing off all educated guesses.

Volcanology is a young and inexact science. "A long-quiet volcano could still take an area by surprise," states Chris Newhall, a volcanologist with the United States Geological Survey.

bles spatter the lava. Often violent, the eruption ejects lava bombs, and sometimes pieces of the volcano's cone itself. Repeated strombolian eruptions from a single volcanic vent can build an enormous shield or composite volcano. More commonly, a strombolian eruption creates a cinder cone.

Vulcanian eruptions happen when a composite volcano suddenly bursts into an eruption. The violent nature of these eruptions comes from plugged vents. Gases pushing up the magma pipe explode the plugs open, throwing out fragments of blocky lava, which often roll down the side of the volcano in a massive avalanche. Mount Shasta formed through vulcanian eruptions, as did Vulcano, in Italy.

Peléean eruptions occur when a composite or dome volcano forms a hard plug of lava inside its main vent. Gases and magma build up pressure behind the plug. Eventually, the plug pops out like a cork. Named for Mount Pelée in Martinique, these eruptions are highly explosive and unpredictable. The eruption may throw a column of hot gas and ash thousands of feet into the air. When this column collapses, it pours down the volcano's side as a pyroclastic flow—a fast and fiery landslide of lava, gas, and dust that incinerates everything in its path.

Plinian eruptions, named for historian Pliny the Younger, explode with a cannonlike bang. Gassy, viscous magma inside the vent shoots upward at high velocity, creating an enormous ash cloud. Like Mount Vesuvius, these powerful eruptions eject streams of ash and pumice high into the atmosphere and generate pyroclastic flows. A large plinian eruption can devastate thousands of square miles.

Beneath the blue waves of the South Pacific, near Vanuatu, lies a volcanic crater dubbed Kuwae. From end to end, the crater is 7 miles (11 kilometers) wide. To create a crater this size, geologists explain, the volcano exploded with a force equal to 2 million atomic bombs. Historical research set the eruption date at the year 1453, because countries worldwide experienced bad harvests that year. The culprit? Millions of cubic feet of volcanic dust from Kuwae, blown into the upper atmosphere, floating around the world, affected the weather.

On the other side of the planet, the city of Constantinople (now Istanbul), capital of the Byzantine Empire, lay under siege by Turkish invaders. Unusual weather patterns brought unseasonable thunderstorms with hail and drenching rains.

A lunar eclipse plunged Constantinople into darkness on May 22. For the next four days, a blanket of heavy fog covered the city. As the fog lifted, people saw strange lights flickering on domed buildings and windows. Flames danced in the sky around the city's grandest church, the Hagia Sophia. Frightened by these omens, the defenders lost faith and allowed Constantinople to fall to the invaders.

FLYING THE DUSTY SKIES

Volcanic dust poses a massive danger to aircraft. In just fifteen years, more than eighty jet aircraft suffered damage from volcanic ash. Since a Boeing 747 costs at least $167 million dollars to replace, repairing the damage is an expensive proposition. It cost more than $80 million dollars to repair the aircraft damaged during KLM Flight 867, including replacing all the engines. Volcanic dust clogs jet intakes, damages sensitive engine parts, drifts into cabins, and erodes glass and metal surfaces—even if the plane is sitting on the runway.

The problem grows larger in certain parts of the world, such as over the North Pacific Ocean. More than 10,000 passengers fly through this zone daily, where plumes of volcanic ash reach the upper atmosphere at least four days a year. At the same time as the KLM incident, four other aircraft suffered catastrophic failures caused by the ash plume of the Redoubt volcano. Since Alaska contains forty-four of the fifty-six or so volcanoes in the United States that have been known to erupt, the Alaska Volcano Observatory was established in 1988. Although it didn't have enough equipment in place at the time to warn the 1989 KLM flight, it now monitors all the North Pacific volcanoes from Alaska across the Aleutian strait into Asia.

The NOAA (National Oceanic and Atmospheric Administration, which tracks weather patterns over North America) and the FAA (Federal Aviation Administration, responsible for air traffic in the United States) work in conjunction with the observatory to detect and track ash clouds in the upper atmosphere. Pilots receive warnings to avoid certain zones while flying. In 1992, the FAA rerouted Trans-Pacific flights around the Arctic Circle because of an ash cloud created by the Spurr volcano in Alaska. Making flying the North Pacific safer, the work of the Alaska Volcano Observatory saves lives and saves money. The entire program will run for fifty years for the cost of replacing a single Boeing 747.

Did the eruption of Kuwae cause the terrible weather and unusual atmospheric effects in Constantinople that changed the course of history? Some scientists and historians think so, because of the nature of volcanic dust.

Volcanic dust is a fine, lightweight dust that can stay suspended in the atmosphere for years. Because of this, volcanic dust affects weather around the world. Dust from a single volcano can travel

*Mount Redoubt, Alaska, has erupted several times
in the last hundred years.*

25

all the way around the world in high atmospheric currents. The massive eruption of Indonesia's Mount Tambora in 1815 caused "the year without a summer" in the United States. Crops couldn't grow because the weather never got warm: it snowed in June, July, and August! And when Krakatau erupted in 1883, the dust it threw into the atmosphere caused brilliant, fiery sunsets around the world for the next seven years.

Volcanic dust can also disrupt air traffic. In 1989, on its way to Anchorage, KLM Flight 867 passed through an enormous cloud spewed by Alaska's Redoubt volcano. The engines failed—all four of them. Sulfur fumes and a thick "smoke" (actually volcanic ash) filled the cabin. Terrified, the passengers watched helplessly as the jet fell more than 2 miles (3.2 kilometers), engines silent. Fortunately, the crew was able to restart the engines at a lower altitude. They landed safely at Anchorage, despite damage to instruments and visual difficulties caused by the "sandblasting" of their windshield by the dust.

The plain between Mount St. Helens and Spirit Lake lies buried under a layer of pumice and ash.

WHAT SPEWS FROM A VOLCANO

As gas-laden magma rises through the pipes inside of a volcano, it becomes bubbly. When this frothy mix spills out on the earth's surface, we call it lava. Depending on the amount and size of bubbles in the lava, and the size and shape of the lava as it falls, it can be classified under many different names.

Unlike the ash that comes from burning wood, **volcanic ash** is

BLACK SMOKERS

In 1977, oceanographers scouring the floor of the Pacific Ocean discovered small volcanolike structures in the ocean depths near the Galápagos Islands. In 1985, another group of researchers found the same strange formations east of Florida in the Atlantic Ocean. They called these eerie undersea pipes black smokers, because they look a lot like chimneys. Black smokers spew out hot mineral-rich water—up to 572°F (300°C)—that sends billowing "clouds" into the surrounding water. Not all black smokers are black. Depending on the mineral content, these hydrothermal vents puff out white, gray, and clear material as well.

Clusters of unusual sea life gather around black smokers. Bacteria feed on manganese and sulfur coming out of the vent. In turn, tubeworms and giant clams gather to feed on the bacteria. Building up skinny smokestack cones made of mineral precipitated from the hot water, these hydrothermal formations grow up to 33 feet (10 meters) tall.

The fluid coming out of these black smoker hydrothermal vents is rich in sulfur and supports a special kind of extremophile bacteria.

made of sharp particles of fragmented lava, like scouring powder. This fine dust easily floats on air currents. When thrown high into the atmosphere as a volcanic plume during an eruption, the dust can travel vast distances. In less than three days, the ash cloud from the 1991 eruption of Mount Pinatubo in the Philippines drifted more than 5,000 miles (8,047 kilometers), raining down on the east coast of Africa. Volcanic ash, or dust, includes any particles less than 2 millimeters (0.7 inch) across.

Scoria occurs when clots of lava cool in midair. Depending on the size of the scoria, it can end up as tiny cinders (scoria made of heavy basalt) or **lapilli** (Italian for "little stones.") Lapilli are pieces of solidified lava, ranging from the size of a peppercorn to the size of a peach—2 to 64 millimeters (0.7 to 2.5 inches) across.

Pumice looks like a rocky sponge when it hardens, but it also starts out as lava. As magma rises from chambers deep within the earth, it reaches a point where its gas content becomes bubbly. The more the bubbly magma rises, the foamier it gets—like the froth coming out of a shaken-up bottle of soda pop. When the volcano erupts, the extremely foamy portion of the magma solidifies into pumice in midair. The quantity of air bubbles in a piece of pumice gives it its unusual character. It's the only rock that can float.

In 1878, masses of pumice covered the sea around the Solomon Islands after an underwater volcano exploded. The floating chunks of rock accumulated like ice floes in bays and harbors, making it almost impossible for ships to move. The bobbing carpet of rock was so thick that people tried to walk on it!

When the volcano spits out a large mass of lava (or an old rock covered with a skin of fresh lava) it creates a **lava bomb**. Lava bombs can be thick in the middle and thin at the ends. Some large bombs have odd-shaped, twisted ends. Almond bombs rotate rapidly in the air, and spin into spindlelike shapes. Breadcrust bombs have a bizarre cracked crust, like a loaf of fresh-baked bread. This happens when the core of a bomb continues to ex-

This accretionary lava ball is about 2.5 feet (75 centimeters) long. It built up like a snowball rolling downhill, picking up more lava as it traveled.

pand after the crust solidifies. Lava bombs include chunks more than 64 millimeters (2.5 inches) long.

When a volcano erupts, it also shatters and crushes the rock in its pipes. These huge blocks of rock tear off the walls and crater of the volcano as it shakes and sputters. During an explosion, a volcano can spit out rocks bigger than houses. The violent explosion may also pulverize some of these rocks, spewing out smaller fragments and dust.

If magma rising through a volcano nears groundwater, the volcano may explode in a burst of steam, called a phreatic explosion. Two months before Mount St. Helens erupted, it sent a plume of steam and ash several thousand feet in the air, blasting out a large crater in the mountain.

FOUNTAINS OF "FIRE"

In Hawaii, enormous fire fountains dance across the night sky. Jets of gas escaping from lava create these colorful explosions from shield or fissure volcanoes. Bright glowing red lava rides in clots and globs along the gas jets. While they commonly jump up

In this view of the July 22, 1980, Mount St. Helens eruption, the steam in the foreground is rising from a pyroclastic flow rushing down the north side of the volcano.

Pele's Hair covering a slope in Hawaii

to about 600 feet (183 meters), fire fountains can shoot up to 1,500 feet (457 meters) high. Fresh lava is thrown into the air constantly. The lava that falls back down ends up as part of the overall lava flow. Sometimes an entire row of fire fountains along a fissure creates a curtain of "fire."

Pele's Hair, also known as rock wool, is a fine bundle of "glass" fibers that forms only in fire fountains. Liquid lava blobs may stretch thin as they fly through the air, like pulled taffy. These thin strands of lava harden in the air. If they are thrown clear of the lava jet, they will survive as a unique "hairy" rock.

SPATTERING AND SPLATTERING: VOLCANIC GROWTH

Tapping deep into a magma chamber, a volcano grows by spitting, spattering, and spewing lava and solid rocks. This accumulation of debris builds a cone around the volcano's main vent. While the main vent carries the force of each eruption, side vents sometimes also spew lava, building up the sides of the volcano. Many of the world's largest volcanoes have composite cones—a cumulative combination of layers of ash and cinders, lava flows, and spattered lava.

Inside the cone, the crater is the cup-shaped depression in the middle, surrounding a vent. A crater is relatively small, and is created when the volcano blasts material out of the vent. A caldera, on

NO SMOKING!

Volcanoes don't smoke. Steam, gas, and vapors rise from the chimney and fumaroles on the volcano's surface, but volcanoes never, ever smoke. Rocks don't burn—they melt. Although lava may look like it's on fire, volcanoes don't belch fire, either. The severe heat—up to 2,400°F (1,300°C)—makes lava glow. Lava, made up of melted rocks and gases, turns to rock as it cools in air or water.

The air around hot lava, however, is so hot that it can cause its surroundings—grass, trees, even buildings—to catch on fire.

Hot lava gushes from a volcano, pouring over a ledge.

the other hand, happens when the cone collapses into the magma chamber below. Compared to a crater, a caldera (Spanish for "cauldron") is huge—like an upside-down volcano.

Calderas sometimes contain other formations dependent on a magma chamber: boiling springs, fumaroles, and lava lakes. Crater lakes form when a caldera fills with water. The deepest lake in North America is inside a caldera—Crater Lake, Oregon. The lake is 2,000 feet (600 meters) deep and 5.6 miles (9 kilometers) in diameter.

Spatter cones grow when the volcano spits out lots of clots of hot lava. These spatter around the vent and cool. The cone grows higher as more spattered clots pile up on top of old, cooled clots.

During an eruption, cinder cones form as ash settles around the vent. During an active eruption, a cinder cone can grow hundreds of feet high in just a few days. One such rapidly growing volcano in Mexico, Paricutin, popped up in a cornfield in 1943. It grew 33

This lava fountain from Mauna Ulu, in Hawaii, in 1969, was 1,492 feet (455 meters) high.

Crater Lake, in Oregon, fills the caldera of Mount Mazama, an extinct volcano.

feet (10 meters) in one day, 450 feet (137 meters) in its first week, and over 1,000 feet (305 meters) in two months!
While cinder cone volcanoes spit out lava as fountains and bombs, shield volcanoes pour out lava that oozes and flows down the sides of the volcano.

3
GASES AND GLOP

GOOEY, GLOPPY LAVA

Wrinkly **pahoehoe** lava oozes in big ropy globs. Its edges are thin. But despite its sluggish look, it moves fast. The "toe," or leading edge of the lava flow, bulges out ahead of the rest of the flow. Pahoehoe cools quickly on the surface, freezing the rock in place. But beneath this deceptive crust, the lava continues to flow.

Aa is lava that flows like a hot stream, carrying along blocks of hardened lava that can weigh as much as several tons. When aa cools, its surface is rough and jagged, easily ripping apart the soles of shoes.

Block lava is similar to aa, but it is stronger and thicker. It looks a lot like broken pavement. Block lava moves slowly, only 3.28 to 16.4 feet (1 to 5 meters) a day. As it cools, its broken surface is studded with angular blocks of lava with smooth faces.

Fissure volcanoes ooze out seas of molten basalt, known as **sheet lava**. Although sheet lava created many vast plains in prehistoric times, the only such eruption in modern history happened in 1783, in Iceland. A sudden and massive upwelling of magma—15 miles (24 kilometers) long—oozed out of the Laki fissure, one of the most frightening events ever in human history. Over eight months, the fissure poured forth 218 square miles (564 square kilometers) of lava, three stories deep. The intense heat from this sea of lava created an unusual dense, dry fog (mostly carbon dioxide) that settled over Europe. Gases seeping from the lava poisoned 75 percent of all the livestock in Iceland. At least 20 percent of the island's population—10,000 people—died because of the resulting famine.

Pillow lava forms at the bottom of the sea, from magma escaping through undersea rifts. The quick chilling of the lava creates odd formations that look like pillows, long and pinched at the ends, stacked against one another.

LAVA AVALANCHES

The most dangerous volcanic burst is a pyroclastic flow (Greek for "broken fire"). Also known by the French term *nuées ardentes* ("glowing clouds"), these mixtures of hot gases and ash roll along the ground at high speeds and with intense heat—up to 1500°F (815°C). A pyroclastic flow is sudden and destructive, pouring down a mountainside at an average speed of 124 miles (200 kilometers) per hour.

Archaeologists believe that the ancient Roman city of Herculaneum, destroyed by the eruption of Mount Vesuvius in A.D. 79, was the victim of a pyroclastic flow. The evidence? Near the shore lay a mass of more than a hundred skeletons of people trying to flee the city. This was an important find for archaeologists, since the Romans believed in cremating (burning) the dead rather than burying them. Studying these skeletons has told archeologists a lot about the life of the early Romans.

The first modern description of a pyroclastic flow came from observers of the 1902 eruption of Mount Pelée in Martinique. The air became "a hurricane of flame," said one of the two survivors.

St. Pierre, a city of 30,000 people, was wiped out in seconds. An inhabitant of a town 5 miles (8 kilometers) away described it as a "terrible suction of air," which tried to drag him toward the volcano, followed by "a sheet of flame that swept toward St. Pierre."

Volcano observers have since paid with their lives by trying to observe and record this deadly phenomenon. On June 3, 1991, a team of three volcanologists and forty journalists climbed Japan's Mount Unzen to film a movie about volcano hazards. An unexpected pyroclastic flow poured over them at more than 200 miles (322 kilometers) per hour, threatening the city of Shimabara below. And after 400 years of quiet, the peak of Soufrière Hills on the island of Montserrat burst forth in a pyroclastic flow on December 26, 1997, destroying dozens of villages that had fortunately been evacuated because of earlier lahars and lava flows.

A lahar is a thick, fast-moving mudflow that happens when a pyroclastic flow mixes with water. Hot lahars occur when the pyroclastic flow explodes through a lake in the volcano's crater. If the pyroclastic flow melts a snowcap on the volcano, the result is a cold lahar. In either case, this muddy mix of lava and water encases everything in its path, and can carry along massive boulders as it rolls downhill at an average speed of 30 miles (48 kilometers) per hour. In 1985, a lahar swept down from Nevado del Ruiz, Colombia, killing 20,000 people by engulfing villages deep in sticky muck.

Rain, soaking into fresh ash, can also create "mud lava." These mudflows are dangerous because the mud is thick and sticky, and can pour rapidly downhill.

BIZARRE LAVA LANDSCAPES

Lava caves often form within pahoehoe flows. This happens when a river of lava crusts over, but continues to flow inside a tube to feed the advancing front of a lava flow. As the eruption quiets, less lava is fed to the tube, and the level of lava starts to drop. Trapped gases become superheated, and they melt the tunnel walls above the lava. As the walls cool, they become glazed like a piece of pottery in a kiln. If lava spurts up into the superheated gas, it will stick to the walls or ceiling of the tube and form a glazed shape: globby grapes, walking sticks, or squirming worms of hardened basalt up to 2 feet (61 centimeters) long. Since the lava river in the bottom of the tube cools at a different rate, the floor of the tube is very different from the walls and ceiling. Lava pouring through these tubes can be as hot as 2,200°F (1,160°C).

Lava lakes are steaming bowls of hot lava, sustained from magma chambers below. In the mountains of Congo National Park, at 11,500 feet (3,505 meters) elevation, is Niragongo, a lava lake that covers more than 35,000 square yards (29,265 square meters). Visitors to the lake say that it forms a transparent, iridescent, plasticlike skin as the lava begins to cool; then the skin breaks and sinks as fresh magma forces its way upward.

The ash is still rising from the Soufrière Hills on the island of Montserrat, and you can see the new shoreline and the pyroclastic flow channel created moments after the eruption.

Ancient lava flows created some unusual geologic features. The incredible basalt columns of the Giant's Causeway in Ireland formed when vast lava sheets cooled slowly, causing the surface of the lava to crackle like dried mud. These hexagonal cracks, called joints, deepened as the lava cooled and shrank in volume, making tall columns in the rock.

Some of the oddly shaped mountains in the Southwestern United States are the eroded remains of ancient volcanic formations. Ship Rock, New Mexico, is a volcanic neck—a chunk of a shallow magma chamber and pipe—as is Devils Tower, Wyoming. And Sunset Crater, Arizona, is a cinder cone.

(Left) Giant's Causeway, on the north coast of Ireland. (Right) Ship Rock, New Mexico

FUMING FORMATIONS

Fumaroles (from the Latin *fumus*, "to smoke") are vents in the earth's surface that sputter volcanic gases and hot steam. They are most often found on and around volcanoes, and in conjunction with geysers. But you don't need a volcano nearby to have fumaroles occur. A pool of magma can be lying beneath a layer of bedrock, as it does in Yellowstone National Park. As vapors rise from the magma pool and pass through the water table, they turn the water to steam, which has a thousand times more volume than water. The fumarole then vents the steam and the vapors at the surface.

Vapors from fumaroles may contain dissolved minerals transported from deep underground. Chemicals in the vapors stain the rocks around fumaroles with colorful patterns. Deposits of stinky yellow sulfur, bright white ammonium chloride, yellow ferrous chloride, and tiny amounts of metals such as iron, zinc, lead, and tin all build up around fumaroles. White calcium carbonate, clear quartz, and yellow and red sodium aluminum sulfates add more touches of color. Some of the most colorful fumaroles are called solfatara, for the Solfatara volcano in Italy. It spits out sulfurous gases and builds up mounds of sulfur around its fumarole vents.

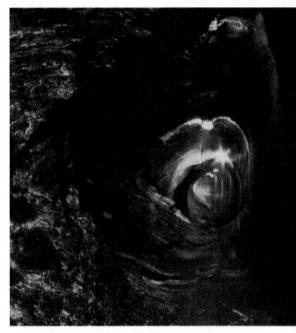

The Thurston Lava Tube, at Kilauea volcano, Hawaii, is roomy—the height near the entrance is 13 feet (4 meters).

During the massive 1912 eruption of the Novarupta volcano on the Alaskan Peninsula, a pyroclastic flow of porous pumice and ash filled a nearby valley 46 square miles (120 square kilometers) up to 660 feet (200 meters) deep. Then the entire valley broke out in fumaroles! These fumaroles sputtered for about fifteen years—the time it took for the valley to cool—then went dormant. Dubbed the Valley of the Ten Thousand Smokes, the area is now part of Katami National Park.

Fumaroles provide warm spots where wildlife gathers. At Yellowstone, bison often cluster around the steamy vents in the middle of winter. The warm air keeps snow at bay for a small radius around the vent, allowing deer, bison, and elk to browse for plants even when the snow is deep elsewhere in the park.

In addition to water vapor and steam, fumaroles and volcanic vents can release toxic gases. Dangerous clouds of carbon dioxide, sulfur dioxide, and hydrogen chloride may emerge without warning. When Iceland's Mount Hekla erupted in 1947, a cloud of carbon dioxide from the explosion settled into low valleys and

Partially hidden by steam from thermal pools, bison graze in Gibbon Meadows in Yellowstone National Park.

depressions, suffocating wandering sheep. In 1997, a group of mountain climbers died when carbon dioxide from Mount Adatara, east of Tokyo, filled their camp. And in 1986, carbon dioxide gases seeped out of Lake Nyos, Cameroon, quietly suffocating 1,700 people living in villages along this African lake.

In California, gases from the Long Valley caldera are killing the forests on the slopes of Mammoth Mountain. Carbon dioxide and methane seep into the soil from the magma body 3 miles (5 kilometers) below the surface, suffocating the roots of the trees.

4
BOIL AND BUBBLE

WARMING UP

Rocks do a great job of holding and transmitting heat from magma. When hot rocks warm up pools of water underground, the water pushes its way upward through fissures and fractures, dissolving minerals from the surrounding rocks. The result is a pool of water called a hot spring.

Unlike normal groundwater emerging in a spring, hot springs contain an odd mix of chemicals. Carbonates and sulphates are common. Many hot springs in the Aegean Islands of Greece contain trace amounts of radium. Through history, these "radioactive" springs have been prized for their curative powers—despite the fact that dosages of radium are unhealthy.

Using natural hot springs, the Romans invented the hot bath. The Roman legions built fifty-seven large bathhouses across their empire. They heated these buildings using hot vapors carried through hollow tiles from nearby hot springs.

As other cultures experimented with hot springs, they used them for medicinal purposes. People would "take the waters" to improve their health, claiming the water would improve skin conditions and lessen the effects of arthritis. In Japan, the on-sen (natural hot springs) are part of Buddhist culture, used for relaxation

Grand Prismatic Spring and the Midway Geyser Basin, in Yellowstone National Park

and restful recharging of the body and spirit. Many spas and expensive resorts in the United States are built around hot springs, such as The Greenbrier at White Sulphur Springs, West Virginia; St. Helena in California's Napa Valley; and Desert Hot Springs in Palm Springs, California.

Although plant life can't tolerate being splashed by hot water, hot springs create a warm microclimate that supports luxurious vegetation. At Yellowstone, bright yellow monkey flowers and yellow fritillary flourish around the boiling springs. Wildlife is attracted to these warm sites as well. Troops of Japanese macaques, the northernmost of all monkeys, live in Japan's volcanic zones.

Also known as snow monkeys, these playful creatures swim and soak in the simmering hot springs.

COMING TO A BOIL

Boiling springs are an intermediate stage between hot springs and geysers. Without the proper conditions to allow it to burst up as a geyser, the water simply rises and falls inside the pool. Sometimes the water will bubble and erupt an inch or two.

The world's largest boiling spring—200 feet (63 meters) across—bubbles atop the isle of Dominica in the Caribbean. Known as Boiling Lake, in Morne Trois Pitons National Park, the grayish-blue water froths and spits out sulfurous vapors from a crater 300 feet (91 meters) deep. And at Yellowstone National Park, the Firehole River is hot running water! Jim Bridger, a settler in the late 1800s, said that the river's water "raced downhill so fast that the river turned warm on the bottom!" But the river is actually warmed by hot springs and geysers all along its course.

As boiling water rises out of the ground, it carries a lot of dissolved material to the surface. In 1777, the court pharmacist of Leopold II, Grand Duke of Tuscany, discovered an interesting chemical in the "lagoni," the hot pools of water common to Tuscany, Italy. The powdery white substance turned out to be boric acid, or borax. It's still used today as a whitener for laundry, and has been mined in many places in the southwestern United States, including Death Valley, California.

As the temperature of superheated water drops, evaporated minerals precipitate or crystallize. So as water rises and cools, the edges of hot springs become coated with beautiful silicate minerals. Colorful varieties of quartz—jasper, agate, chalcedony, and glassy opal—line the edges of each hot pond.

THAR SHE BLOWS!

Geysers are the rarest of all the earth's hot formations. Only eight hundred or so are found on the entire planet. Like fumaroles, geysers don't require a volcano nearby, just the proper heat and

Whakarewarewa, on the North Island of New Zealand, at Rotorua, is a cluster of seven geysers.

plumbing under the earth's surface. These unique vents spit up steam and water on a regular schedule. Old Faithful, in Yellowstone National Park, is the world's best-known geyser, throwing 5,000 gallons (23,000 liters) of water up to 150 feet (45 meters) in the air. It erupts every 75 to 90 minutes—not as often as it used to, but the patterns of geysers tend to change. There are more than 500 known geysers in Yellowstone National Park, more than anywhere else in the world. Coming in second is the

Kronotsky Nature Preserve on Russia's Kamchatka Peninsula, with almost 200 geysers, some as small as 1 inch (2.5 centimeters) tall. Other countries with major geyser fields include Iceland, Chile, and New Zealand.

In 1847, German chemist Robert Wilhelm Bunsen studied the Great Geysir in Iceland, the namesake of all geysers. By 1855, he'd invented the Bunsen burner—which forces air and gas up through a tube, similar to a fumarole.

The word geyser comes from the Icelandic verb *gjose*, "to erupt." In its heyday, the Great Geysir burst over 200 feet (61 meters) into the air. Today, it takes a little priming with laundry soap to encourage the Great Geysir to explode (the soap encourages the superheated water to boil). A neighboring geyser, Strokkur, is now Iceland's largest, throwing a plume of water 50 feet (15.2 meters) into the air several times an hour.

The world's largest known geyser, which is no longer belching, was at Waimangu, New Zealand. Not only would it spit out water, it also threw up stones, carried up and out by the sprays of water. Active between 1900 and 1904, it generated a fountain over 1,000 feet (305 meters) high. Today, the tallest known geyser is Steamboat Geyser in Yellowstone National Park. It throws out a fountain of water from 195 to 380 feet (60 to 115 meters) high.

There are two types of geysers. Fountain geysers rise from within a surface pool of boiling water. Columnar geysers pop out of a dry

Waimangu Geyser, in a photograph from 1904, was only active for four years.

GO, GEYSER, GO!

Geysers are erupting hot springs. A special set of conditions must be in place for a geyser to form: the perfect combination of heat and water, an underground reservoir, and just the right size opening with a pipe feeding it. Add less water or make it hotter, and you get a fumarole. Too much water creates a hot pool. If the water is muddy, a bubbling mud pot forms. If the mud is thick, you get a mud volcano. If the opening is too large, the pool becomes a boiling spring.

A geyser is made up of a reservoir and an opening through which the column of water rises. Initially, the reservoir fills with hot water and gases heated from the magma below. As more water pushes toward the surface, the reservoir gets superheated; the water is now hotter than the boiling point. When the superheated water in the reservoir turns to steam, it's hotter than the water above it in the pipe. The steam pushes the column of water up the pipe into the air. A burst of steam from the reservoir then follows the burst of water from the pipe. The geyser quiets down as the reservoir refills again.

sinter cone, like a small volcano. At Yellowstone, some of the sinter cones look like giant beehives. Colors in the hot pools vary from clear and brilliant blue to yellows and reds caused by heat-loving algae, and ink black water muddied by suspended particles of iron. Geyserite, a mineral created by geyser systems, is a type of opal that forms a natural seal in the underground cooker that generates the geyser.

Sometimes people accidentally create "geysers." The Crystal Geyser at Green River, Utah, now erupts every five hours from a hole drilled by prospectors looking for steam for geothermal energy. The nearby Champagne Geyser erupts ice-cold carbonated water. Neither one is technically a geyser, since they aren't natural springs. Perpetual spouters are like geysers except they constantly erupt, with only a momentary pause between explosions.

Geysers are very sensitive to changes in the environment. Gravitational forces affect how frequently geysers erupt, as does the barometric pressure. Since geysers rely on a unique plumbing system of interconnected channels underground, a single earth tremor can silence a geyser forever. Or a geyser could be silenced by someone drilling a well and tapping off steam or hot water. Geysers also clog up with their own debris. To protect the geysers at Yellowstone, the rangers vacuum some of the geyser pools. They remove natural debris and litter (including coins) that careless visitors toss into the pools.

HOT BUBBLING MUD

Mud pots are hot springs with very little water. The consistency of the mud is dependent on the amount of water; mud pots can be soupy or almost dry. Minerals—mostly iron pyrite—color mud pots gray, white, black, or cream-colored.

Mud pots can be any size, from a tiny hole in the ground to a funnel shape up to 33 feet (10 meters) in diameter and 16.5 feet (5 meters) deep. The outward explosions of mud create bizarre patterns on the surface of a mud pot, like concentric rings and stiff knobs.

Thanks to steam in the water, mud pots bubble and boil. If the gases build up in a viscous mix of mud, a mud pot can belch and spatter its surroundings with boiling mud. Mud volcanoes happen when a mud pot gets hyperactive, spitting huge globs of mud into the sky. The blobs of mud form a cone or mound, forming

A close-up of a spattering mud pot at Pocket Basin, Yellowstone National Park

The glistening white travertine terraces at Pamukkale, Turkey, earned this formation the nickname "Cotton Castle."

the mud volcano. At the Mushpots site in Wyoming's Yellowstone National Park, one large mud volcano churned out globs of mud as big as a cabin. It spewed mud up to 100 feet (30 meters) into the air.

Paint pots are mud pots with style. Colored by additional minerals in the hot water, they glisten in odd shades: blue, orange, red, pink, and yellow. Pink and red paint pots get their color from iron oxide. Sulfur minerals color yellow and orange mud pots.

TERRACES

Hot water dripping from the spray of geysers, or running in a stream from a hot spring, contains a lot of dissolved minerals. When water splashes out of a boiling spring, it coats nearby rocks with layers of silica, creating "geyserite eggs." If the mineral-laden water flows over surfaces, it leaves the minerals behind, forming an ever-growing deposit. These deposits create terraces of stone covered with travertine—flowstone formations similar to those seen inside caverns.

Pamukkale, Turkey, contains one of the world's largest terrace formations—the "Cotton Castle," more than 328 feet (100 meters) high. As water flowed out of the hot springs and down into the river valley, it deposited rich, foamy-looking layers of travertine. These white terraces sparkle in the sunshine.

HOT LANDSCAPES

ICELAND: FIRE AND ICE

Despite its name, Iceland is a fiery country. It straddles the mid-Atlantic ridge, where new land appears as the Eurasian and North American tectonic plates are pushed apart from each other. And Iceland has new land being created every day. In the past 500 years, roughly a third of all the lava erupting on the earth's surface has been in Iceland. The country gains at least 1.5 acres (0.6 hectares) of land every year.

With rifts and fissures, craters and mountains, Iceland is a land of stark geologic beauty. Ice-cold lakes fill sunken valleys and the craters of ancient volcanoes. There are lava deserts, and gigantic waterfalls that flow over basalt cliffs. Geysers spout water, and fumaroles sputter with steam.

Lake Myvatn, in northeastern Iceland, is one of the world's most volcanically active spots. Its lava hills and craters make it look like the surface of the moon—which is why NASA's Apollo 11 astronauts did their lunar training here. Since then, fresh fissures have poured out more lava, and new hot springs, fumaroles, and mud pots have appeared.

Deep fissures in the ground mark where the continental plates pull apart in Thingvellir, a valley to the northeast of Iceland's capital city, Reykjavik. Thingvellir is an imposing place, a narrow, deep valley with steep-sided cliffs. The Vikings gathered at Thingvellir in A.D. 930 to found the Althing, the world's oldest parliament. Every year, the Viking settlers would gather and camp in this long, deep valley for two weeks to settle their grievances, make new laws, swap stories, and enjoy each other's company. In A.D. 1000, the settlers declared their conversion to Christianity while they met in the deep valley. But by 1789, the Parliament Plains had sunk enough to become swampy, so the Althing ended and the parliament moved into a building in Reykjavik. Thingvellir keeps sinking, and its rifts keep tearing. At Thingvellir, the country stretches an average of 0.8 inch (2 centimeters) each year.

Magma flows deep under the landscape of Iceland, connecting rifts and volcanoes up to 45 miles (72 kilometers) apart. With more than twenty active volcanoes, eruptions and lava flows are a way of life. At least one volcano erupts every five years. These fiery forces create astounding landscapes, and sometimes give birth to new islands—like Surtsey, south of Iceland. In 1973, the island of Heimaey, a major fishing port, dealt with the eruption of the Helgafell volcano. Five months of spewing lava and falling ash added an extra square mile (2.6 square kilometers) to the island, but demolished three hundred homes, burying them under ash fall. When a lava flow threatened the harbor, the townspeople pumped seawater into fire hoses and hosed down the hot lava. For 155 days they fought the lava, slowing its progress. One third of the town was lost, but the harbor was saved.

Mount Hekla is Iceland's most active volcano, erupting at least twenty-four times in recorded history. After its eruption in 1104, visiting Irish monks called it a gateway to hell. Its unique location on top of a system of faults across the two continental plates may be the reason for its frequent activity, since earthquakes along the plates constantly jostle the magma pipes. The busy tectonic movement of the mid-Atlantic ridge feeds magma to these faults.

Fire and ice meet under Iceland's glaciers, which cover nearly 10 percent of the island. Author Jules Verne used the Snæfellsjökull glacier as his gateway to a new world in *Journey to*

These two photographs are of the Bárôarbunga volcano erupting beneath Vatnajökull glacier in 1996. The photo on the left shows the path the jökulhlaup traveled.

the Center of the Earth. It sits atop a dormant volcano. But when one of these volcanoes erupts under a glacier—watch out!

The Vikings first wrote about the "giant flood," the *jökulhlaup,* in their twelfth-century sagas. In the fall of 1996, modern Icelanders got to experience it firsthand. Buried deep beneath Europe's largest glacier, Vatnajökull, the Bárôarbunga volcano erupted. It took two months for the hot lava to melt the glacier beneath its icy cap. When the water broke free, it raged toward the sea at a rate peaking at 1,678 miles (2,700 kilometers) per hour. It washed away parts of three bridges, including Iceland's longest bridge, the 2,953-foot (900-meter) long Skeiôará bridge along Iceland's critical coastal road. *Jökulhlaups* have happened before at Vatnajökull, creating a unique sandy plain along the south coast of Bárôarbunga.

With people on hand to watch these geologic events since A.D. 900, Iceland has excellent records of the shaping of its country by the forces of the earth. Art and literature celebrate the perpetual change of the Icelandic landscape—where magma is always on the go.

YELLOWSTONE: GEOLOGY AT PLAY

Few people believed the tales explorers and trappers told as they struggled back from the Wyoming Territory in the early 1800s. Bubbling mud in dozens of colors! Fountains of water that suddenly exploded into the sky! Boiling rivers! "Paint cannot touch it, and words are wasted," wrote artist Frederic Remington in 1895.

When the Washburn Expedition visited Yellowstone in 1870, they were quite stunned at what they found. Wrote one explorer, Nathaniel P. Langford, "This new field of wonders . . . should be set apart as a public National Park for the enjoyment of the American people for all time." The photos the expedition brought back helped them convince a doubtful Congress to make Yellowstone the very first national park in the United States. Langford became its superintendent.

Yellowstone sits in several ancient collapsed cal-

Old Faithful, in
Yellowstone National Park

deras. A reservoir of hot water sits atop the magma pool, always at least 8 miles (5 kilometers) below the surface. The park contains more "hot stuff" than anywhere else on earth—at least ten thousand thermal features, including geysers, mud pots, hot springs, and fumaroles. Creeks rise and fall with the variations in the underground plumbing system, as thousands of fumaroles and geysers shoot hot water and steam into the air. Pressure from magma makes the entire caldera "breathe"—five times in the past nine thousand years, according to geologists—lifting and lowering the water levels in Yellowstone Lake.

Geology is fun to watch at Yellowstone. The soupy Fountain Paint Pots burp and bubble, generating spreading rings of yellow and orange. Silex Spring suddenly clouds with a burst of steam from a natural jet in its side, like a Jacuzzi. With 1,350 square miles (3,495 square kilometers) of thermal activity in the caldera, there are dozens of geyser basins to explore. Every geyser has its own unique behavior. The Fountain Geyser explodes wildly in every direction. Jet Geyser spits out of five different vents all at once. Great Fountain starts as a bubbling pool of water that pushes a column of water into the sky. Whirligig Geyser chugs as it erupts. Pools of boiling water glimmer in a dozen colors. Vapors rise from warm rivers.

After a visit to the valley, the naturalist John Muir wrote, in 1898, "A thousand Yellowstone wonders are calling, 'Look up, and down, and 'round about you!'"

6 HARNESSING THE HEAT

Volcanoes and volcanic formations serve as reminders that we live atop a cauldron of explosive energy, a powerful force that builds mountains and shapes valleys. While volcanic activity destroys landscapes, it also creates new, fertile land. The fiery forces raging beneath the earth's surface provide us with a natural source of energy—geothermal energy.

Geothermal energy is a reliable source of energy in regions where the constant output of hot steam or hot water is assured by a pool of hot magma—or rocks conducting and storing heat from distant pools of magma—below the earth's surface. When magma heats rocks surrounding reservoirs of water, the water rises to the surface as hot springs or geysers, or as steam in fumaroles. This resource can be tapped by drilling "steam wells" into the hot ground.

Advanced civilization is not a requirement for utilizing geothermal energy. The Maori of New Zealand have used it for centuries, cooking and washing in the hot springs of the valley of Whakarewarewa. And from Iceland's earliest days, settlers learned that they could use permanently hot ground as a cheap oven. They put bread dough in a tin mold, covered it with hot earth, and came back a few hours later to find a steaming, warm loaf of bread! The settlers also planted their crops in warm ground, where vegetables would grow quickly.

Iceland is the only country in the world that relies heavily on geothermal energy. The name of the capital city, Reykjavik, means "Bay of Steam." Today, the Icelanders pipe hot water (302° to 356°F, or 150° to 180°C) from geothermal fields across the countryside. Hot water and steam provide heat to 85 percent of Iceland's homes. Steam is used for drying salt and drying fish. Warm water provides the environment needed for growing crops out of season; tomatoes and bananas are harvested year-round in Icelandic greenhouses. People even swim outdoors in the middle of winter, enjoying pools heated with naturally hot water.

Iceland's Svartsengi geopower station rises behind the Blue Lagoon, where you can see bathers at the right.

Pioneering the use of geothermal energy for power generation, the Italians started using natural steam vents to heat boilers in 1897. By 1952, they generated 6 percent of their country's electricity using steam-driven turbines in Tuscany. By pumping cold water into hot ground, steam-driven electrical plants run on the steam that shoots back up out of the ground and into pipes leading to the turbines. Using steam, the Italians now provide electricity for almost 600,000 people. They also use hot water to directly heat homes and greenhouses. Small amounts of water from warm sedimentary rock basins in France, Germany, Switzerland, and Austria are pumped out and used to keep houses warm.

Countries along the Pacific "ring of fire" are trying to use geothermal heat to their advantage. Japan is the world's largest user of geothermal heat. There, more than 14,000 geothermal wells have been drilled to tap steam for use in agriculture and in tourist resorts, and to provide hot baths. Vast reservoirs of heat under the Philippines are tapped to provide electricity for almost 1.4 million people. Residents of the Philippines also use geothermal heat for fish processing, salt production, and drying fruit. In nearby Indonesia, steam turbines provide electricity for 300,000 people. New Zealand taps steam fields in the Taupo volcanic zone (over 124 miles, or 200 kilometers, long) to heat houses and to generate electric power, to dry crops and to dry wood pulp in a paper mill. Hot water provides year-round bathing and keeps greenhouses warm. In Canada, geothermal heat keeps water pipes from freezing in the Yukon.

The United States has the world's largest geothermal energy plant—the Geysers, in California. Ninety miles (145 kilometers) north of San Francisco, it covers 15 acres (6 hectares). From a handful of steam wells drilled in 1960, the complex grew to more than 200 steam wells and twelve generating plants. Using steam-driven turbines, the Geysers generates enough power to provide 3.5 million California residents with electricity. Geothermal energy plants in Hawaii, Utah, and Nevada generate enough power for 250,000 people. In other places across the West, geothermal steam wells provide heat for office buildings and greenhouses.

GLOSSARY

aa: lava surface composed of jagged angular blocks.

ash: sharp, fine particles of crushed rock blown out of a volcanic vent.

avalanche: a large mass of material falling or sliding down a sloped surface.

basalt: the most common volcanic rock, usually dark and rich in iron and magnesium.

block: a large chunk of rock, usually 3 feet (1 meter) or more across, thrown out of a volcano during an eruption.

bomb: lava fragment ejected from a volcano, 2.5 inches (64 millimeters) or larger in length.

caldera: a large depression, more than 1 mile (1.6 kilometers) across, created by an explosive collapse of the top of a volcano.

cone: pile of hardened lava and cinders at the top of a volcano, around a vent.

crater: a steep-walled depression at the top of a cone.

dome: a steep-sided mass of thick lava extruded around a volcanic vent like toothpaste from a tube.

fissure: a crack or fracture in the ground.

fumarole: a vent that emits volcanic gases and steam.

geothermal: having to do with heat from the earth.

geyser: a hot spring that periodically erupts into a fountain, followed by a gush of steam or gases.

hot spot: site of a permanent magma pipe rising to the earth's surface.

hydrothermal: having to do with hot water.

igneous: rocks that result from the cooling of molten rock.

lahar: a torrential flow of water-soaked volcanic debris, similar to a mudslide.

lapilli: small fragments of hardened lava ejected from a volcano.

lava: mixture of gases and magma ejected from a volcanic vent.

lithosphere: the outer part of the earth, made of rock, usually 50 miles (80 kilometers) thick.

magma: molten rock beneath the earth's surface.

mantle: the region of the earth lying between the lithosphere and the earth's solid core.

opal: a silica mineral, containing water, that precipitates from hot water.

pahoehoe: basalt lava with a ropy surface.

Pele's hair: cooled thin strands of lava from a fire fountain.

pumice: pale-colored, spongy-looking volcanic rock that is sometimes light enough to float on water.

pyroclastic: any material explosively ejected from a volcano.

pyroclastic flow: a hot mass of gases and volcanic debris that speeds down the side of a volcano; also called *nuée ardente*.

scoria: dark-colored spongy-looking volcanic rock formed from rough lava that cools as it flies through the air.

seamount: a submarine volcano.

sinter: any type of hot spring mineral deposit, regardless of chemical composition.

tectonic plates: the immense floating fragments of the earth's surface that, according to the theory of plate tectonics, move in relation to each other, creating new land and causing earthquakes and volcanoes to erupt.

travertine: an aboveground mineral deposit created by calcium carbonate left behind when warm, mineral-rich water flows over other surfaces.

tsunami: a large "tidal wave" caused by volcanic eruptions and earthquakes.

vent: an opening on the earth's surface that spews volcanic materials.

FURTHER READING

Benson, Marjorie. *Yellowstone*. (Wonders of the World). Austin TX: Raintree/Steck Vaughn, 1995.

Gallant, Roy A. *Geysers: When Earth Roars*. Danbury CT: Watts, 1998.

George, Jean Craighead. *Dear Katie, The Volcano Is a Girl*. New York: Hyperion Press, 1998. (fiction)

Jacobs, Linda. *Letting Off Steam: The Story of Geothermal Energy*. Minneapolis: Carolrhoda Books, 1990.

Lampton, Christopher F. *Volcano*. Brookfield CT: Millbrook Press, 1994.

Lasky, Kathryn. *Surtsey: The Newest Place on Earth*. New York: Hyperion Press, 1992.

Lauber, Patricia. *Volcano: The Eruption and Healing of Mount St. Helens*. New York: Simon & Schuster, 1993. Aladdin Paperbacks.

Lepthien, Emilie U. *Iceland*. (Enchantment of the World). Danbury CT: Children's Press, 1987.

Rice, Christopher, and Melanie Rice. *Pompeii: The Day a City Was Buried*. New York: DK Publishing, 1998.

Silverstein, Alvin, Virginia Silverstein, and Laura Silverstein Nunn. *Plate Tectonics*. Brookfield CT: Twenty-First Century Books, 1998.

Tanaka, Shelley. *The Buried City of Pompeii: What It Was Like When Vesuvius Exploded*. New York: Disney Press, 1997.

Thomas, Margaret. *Volcano!* (Nature's Disasters). Columbus OH: Crestwood House, 1991.

WORLD WIDE WEB

These Web sites contain a lot of information on "hot" geologic topics. You can dig a little deeper by using a search engine and trying out keywords like "volcano," "fumarole," "magma," "geyser," "mud pot," and "hot springs."

MTU Volcanoes Page
http://www.geo.mtu.edu/volcanoes/
Contains "Earth's Active Volcanoes by Geographic Region," a list of links to information on every active volcano in the world, along with detailed information on current eruptions. From the Keweenaw Volcano Observatory, MichiganTechnological University.

The Volcanic Homepage
http://www.aist.go.jp/GSJ/~jdehn/v-home.htm
Contains animations modeling volcanic eruptions, and interesting photos of volcanoes and volcanic landforms. By Dr. Jonathan Dehn of the Geologic Survey of Japan.

Volcano World
http://volcano.und.nodak.edu/
A comprehensive Web site covering volcanoes, active and dormant, around the world. Includes video clips, images, information on volcano observatories and parks—even extraterrestrial volcanoes! Sponsored by NASA Learning Technologies Project.

Volcanoes Online
http://hyperion.advanced.org/17457/
An educational Web site with games, quizzes, and information on the formation of volcanoes and volcanic features. Created by a team of students who participated in the 1998 Thinkquest contest.

USGS Cascades Volcano Observatory
http://vulcan.wr.usgs.gov/
Information on volcanoes, volcanic formations, and their hazards.
Focusing on the Cascades Range in Washington, Oregon, and California.
From the United States Geological Survey.

WyoJones' Geyser Site
http://www.web-net.com/jonesy/geysers.htm
A Wyoming resident with a love of geysers put together this Web site featuring the geysers of Yellowstone. Includes general information on the how and why of geysers, and links to other geyser pages.

Yellowstone Net Geyser Information
http://www.yellowstone.net/geysers/
Beautiful photos and an overview of all the thermal features—geysers, fumaroles, mud pots, hot springs—in Yellowstone National Park. Includes maps of the geyser basins. By geyser fan David Monteith.

INDEX